GOING OUT,
GETTING DUMPED,
and Playing Mini Golf on the First Date

by Tim Pauls

CONCORDIA PUBLISHING HOUSE · SAINT LOUIS

Published by Concordia Publishing House
3558 S. Jefferson Avenue
St. Louis, MO 63118-3968
www.cph.org 1-800-325-3040

Library of Congress Cataloging-in-Publication Data
Pauls, Tim, 1967-
Going out, getting dumped, and playing mini golf on the first date/
by Tim Pauls.
    p. cm.
ISBN 0-7586-0833-0
1. Single people -- Conduct of life. 2. Dating (Social customs)
-- Religious aspects--Christianity. I. Title.
BV4596.S5P38   2005
241'.6765--dc22

                                          2005016615

1 2 3 4 5 6 7 8 9 10   14 13 12 11 10 09 08 07 06 05

For Teresa

With thanks
to our Lord for
thirteen years
of marriage and
the ongoing
pursuit of a
date that
actually goes
according to plan.
It could still
happen.

Table of Contents

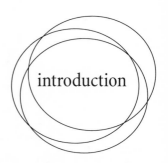
introduction

Welcome to the Weird World of Dating

Want some good, godly information about dating? Don't we all! When I set out to put together this study for youth I checked out the World Wide Web to see what's already available. Now, usually, you can find some agreement out there, but when it comes to dating, each Web site seems extraordinarily different from the rest. It's hard even to sum up what they're saying.

Of course, this book isn't based upon the thoughts of other people. Since, as Christians, we look first and foremost at what the Bible has to say. In this case, that's a little difficult, too. Why? Because dating, as we know it today, didn't exist in Bible times. When we look to scriptural texts on courtship, here's the sort of stuff that we find:

There's the time that the tribe of Benjamin ran out of women (Judges 21). Their solution was for the men to go to Shiloh and hide in the vineyard. Each one would grab a woman who came out to dance in the vineyard during the festival and marry her. We have a word for this in our present day: Kidnapping! I wouldn't recommend this as a 21st century dating technique.

Then there's Deuteronomy 21, which says that a soldier may marry a war bride as long as he shaves the woman's head, trims her nails, and then leaves her alone for a month. I don't advise this one, either.

Ruth uncovered Boaz's feet and slept by them for the night (Ruth 3:7). The two later tied the knot. In our present age, I've got to vote against this one, too.

In biblical times, marriages were usually arranged by the parents for their children—*period*—end of discussion. Remember Isaac? His father, Abraham, sent a trusted servant to find a bride for Isaac:

> *"I came today to the spring and said, 'O LORD, the God of my master Abraham, if now you are prospering the way that I go, behold, I am standing by the spring of water. Let the virgin who comes out to draw water, to whom I shall say, "Please give me a little water from your jar to drink," and who will say to me, "Drink, and I will draw for your camels also," let her be the woman whom the LORD has appointed for my master's son.' Before I had finished speaking in my heart, behold, Rebekah came out with her water jar on her shoulder, and she went down to the spring and drew water. I said to her, 'Please let me drink.' She quickly let down her jar from her shoulder and said, 'Drink, and I will give your camels drink also.' So I drank, and she gave the camels drink also."*
> GENESIS 24:42–46

From start to finish, it was up to the parents. Of course, if they could find you a beautiful virgin who would even water your camels, more power to 'em.

Do you see what I'm getting at? There's no chapter in the Bible entitled "Commands for Dating and Courtship." Frankly, the Bible does not speak directly to the matter of contemporary dating. Nowhere in the Bible do you find advice about going out for pizza and a movie. The Lord did not fail to anticipate dating, but He did decline to address it specifically in His holy Word.

However, the Bible does teach us a lot that we can apply to the subject of dating, so we're not left completely clueless. Although the Lord's proclamation of Law and Gospel doesn't mention dating in particular, it still applies. So here's the plan: We're going to talk about dating and related subjects in light of God's Word—Law and Gospel.

This book is *not* going to tell you the best hot spots in town for a date or advise you on fresh breath and conquering body odor—which is a very good idea. Nor will this book let you know whether or not paisley goes with plaid on your outfit. (It doesn't.) If that's what you're hoping for, you're going to be disappointed. Besides, the last thing you want is *me* telling *you* what's fun on a date. I'm a pastor, married with two kids. A big night out for us is the local burger joint, wondering how many infectious germs our boys are picking up inside the play structure. Anyway, this book is not about stuff like that. Instead, it's going to give you some basic Law and Gospel that should govern your relationships with members of the opposite sex.

God willing, one day you will get married. This

will include dating, getting dumped, and relating to your parents. We'll talk about all of these issues especially as they relate to God's plan for marriage. Since our society is obsessed with sex and wants you to be sexually active long before marriage, we'd better take some time to talk about sex, too.

I've got to take a moment to say thanks to Patty Holm and Pastor Mike McCoy for taking the time to read this and make some helpful comments that make this much better than it otherwise would have been.

Let's get started with this prayer for the youth of the church:

> *God our Father, Your Son grew in wisdom and stature and in favor with God and men. Bless, guide, and govern the children and young people of Your Church by Your Holy Spirit that they may grow in grace and in the knowledge of Your Word. Grant that they may serve You well and usefully, developing their talents not for their own sakes but for the glory of God and the welfare of their neighbor. Protect and defend them from all danger and harm, giving Your holy angels charge over them; through Jesus Christ our Lord. Amen.* "PRAYER FOR YOUNG PERSONS" LUTHERAN WORSHIP P. 127

The Lord be with you!
Pastor Tim Pauls

marriage:
a battlefield
of selfishness
vs. servanthood

chapter

one

chapter one

We're starting with marriage?!

Clearly, this doesn't make sense. First you date, then you marry. Any sensible book about dating is going to follow that order; otherwise, you've got to wonder about the mental state of the author.

I wonder about that, too, but we're going to start with marriage. Why? Because I want to start out with the Bible. I want to lay down a foundation of truth from the Word on which we'll build the rest of this discussion. Remember what we talked about in the introduction: the Bible doesn't talk about dating, and you can't build a foundation on nothing. However, the Bible does talk about marriage, so we've got something to build on.

Marriage is far deeper and more intimate than dating, but both deal with the relationship between a man and a woman. So we're going to start out with a look at the original man and woman, husband and wife—Adam and Eve.

The Perfect Couple

On the sixth day of the Creation, "the LORD God formed the man of dust from the ground and breathed into his nostrils the breath of life, and the man became a living creature" (Genesis 2:7). Adam was placed in the Garden of Eden with the responsibility to keep and tend it (Genesis 2:15). Prior to the creation of Eve, the Lord commanded Adam, "You may surely eat of every tree of the garden, but of the tree of the knowledge of good and evil you shall not eat, for in the day that you eat of it you shall surely die" (Genesis 2:16–17). With this command, the Lord entrusted His Word to Adam. As part of caring for all within the Garden of Eden, Adam was instructed to care for Eve and their future children by telling them the Word of God.

"Then the LORD God said, 'It is not good that the

15

man should be alone; I will make him a helper fit for him'" (Genesis 2:18). Despite what some feminists would tell you, there is no shame to being a helper, nor does it indicate lower status. God calls Himself a helper in Hebrews 13:6, "So we can confidently say, 'The Lord is my helper; I will not fear; what can man do to me?'"

When God created Adam and Eve in His own image (Genesis 1:27), He created them to be helpers and servants like Him. Now, the Bible says that Eve was "comparable," not identical, to Adam. She was different, but the differences between Adam and Eve complemented each other. In other words, God purposely created them differently with different roles, designing them to help and serve one another.

The Lord opened Adam's side and removed a rib from which He created Eve (Genesis 2:21–22). He blessed them in part by saying, "Be fruitful and multiply and fill the earth and subdue it and have dominion over the fish of the sea and over the birds of the heavens and over every living thing that moves on the earth" (Genesis 1:28). With this blessing, the Lord declared that the human population would grow by the birth of children. God could have kept making us out of dirt and ribs if He wanted to, but He entrusted Eve with the privilege of nurturing life by nurturing children. As Adam and Eve served one another, they would also become servants to the children whom the Lord gave them.

Hopefully, you see the theme in Genesis 2—it's one of servanthood. Certainly you've heard of a guy and a gal being called the "perfect couple" or "made for each other"? Both were literally true for Adam and Eve. The perfect husband and wife were perfect servants. Servanthood was the natural, default setting of humankind without sin.

SIN AND SELFISHNESS ARRIVE

Tempted by the serpent, Adam and Eve disobeyed God and fell into sin (Genesis 3:1–7). Scripture lays the blame on both. Eve is faulted for being the first to eat fruit of the tree of the knowledge of good and evil. "Adam was not deceived, but the woman was deceived and became a transgressor" (1 Timothy 2:14). St. Paul declares that sin and death came through Adam,

> *Therefore, just as sin came into the world through one man, and death through sin, and so death spread to all men because all sinned—for sin indeed was in the world before the law was given, but sin is not counted where there is no*

> *law. Yet death reigned from Adam to Moses, even over those whose sinning was not like the transgression of Adam, who was a type of the one who was to come.* ROMANS 5:12–14

Adam, entrusted with the Word of God, failed to keep preaching it to Eve and allowed her to eat. By failing to speak, he failed to serve his bride. The shift from servanthood to selfishness was evident immediately. Adam blamed God and Eve for his eating the fruit, "The woman whom You gave to be with me, she gave me fruit of the tree, and I ate"(Genesis 3:12). Eve passed the blame onto the serpent "The serpent deceived me, and I ate" (Genesis 3:13). Both fell from selfless service to selfish *self*-preservation.

When the Lord spoke after the Fall, He announced curses and consequences. In Genesis 3:15, God declared to Satan that the Seed of the woman would destroy him. While a matter of great consequence for the devil, this is a matter of great promise to us as the first proclamation of the Gospel! Note this well—although Adam and Eve had fallen from servanthood to selfishness, *the Lord remained the perfect Servant.* He immediately promised that His Son would become flesh and suffer death for the sins of the world. His Son would be the suffering Servant wounded for our transgressions and bruised for our iniquities.

> *Behold My servant, whom I uphold, My chosen, in whom My soul delights; I have put My Spirit upon Him; He will bring forth justice to the nations. He will not cry aloud or lift up His voice, or make it heard in the street; a bruised reed He will not break, and a faintly burning wick He will not quench; He will faithfully bring forth justice. He will not grow faint or be discouraged till He has established justice in the earth; and the coastlands wait for His law.*
> ISAIAH 42:1–4

The Lord announced curses and consequences to Adam and Eve, as well. Eve would experience great pain in childbearing, a reminder that all born of man are condemned to pain in life and eventually death. Adam faced far harder labor in the fields, for the earth was infected with sin and would rebel against his efforts. It was a double-whammy: Because of sin in the world, Adam and Eve's daily tasks were going to be a whole lot more difficult. Even worse, because of sin in *them*, they wouldn't want to serve and do those chores anymore—though their survival depended upon it.

For what we're studying, though, note especially

the Lord's final statement of Genesis 3:16. He said to Eve, "Your *desire* shall be for your husband, and he shall *rule* over you." This announcement has often been misinterpreted as establishing man's dominion over women. In other words, some will tell you that they were equals up to then, but now the Lord made Adam the boss and Eve the slave. But look more closely. Rather than repeating the relationship or establishing a new chain of command, the Lord identifies how that relationship would become twisted by sin.

"Your *desire* shall be for your husband, and he shall *rule* over you." What does this mean? Here's an important tip: When a Bible verse is tough to understand, the best thing to do is to see if other verses in the Bible can help us out, either by using the same words or talking about the same subject. In this case, we're in luck. The same words for "desire" and "rule" pop up together a chapter later in Genesis 4:7. At the start of Genesis 4, Cain is angry and jealous of his brother Abel because the Lord accepts Abel's offering. As Cain sulks, the Lord says to him, "If you do well, will you not be accepted? And if you do not do well, sin is crouching at the door. Its desire is for you, but you must rule over it."

Look at how similar the structure of these verses is:

Your **desire** shall be for your husband, and he shall **rule** over you (Genesis 3:16).

Its **desire** is for you, but you must **rule** over it (Genesis 4:7).

We note the similarity because the context of Genesis 4:7 helps us understand the meaning of Genesis 3:16. Clearly, the desire of sin was to move Cain to disobedience—to reject the plan that God had for him. Therefore, Cain was to rule over it—overpower it, control it and keep it in its place.

We conclude that, in Genesis 3:16, the Lord was declaring how sin would pervert and twist the relationship between Adam and Eve, between men and women. So, what was Eve's sinful desire for her husband? Because of sin, she would naturally reject the plan that God had for the sexes, desiring to change the roles He ordained for man and woman. Rather than serve Adam, Eve would want him to serve her. Because of sin, Adam would likewise reject God's plan and naturally work to "rule over" Eve—to overpower her, control her and keep her "in her place."

Note that the Lord did not approve of either of these behaviors; rather, He was announcing how sin would undermine the relationship. Rather than live as servants to one another, Adam and Eve would now seek to be served—to look out for themselves at the expense of others. This consequence of sin will continue to carry itself out in the "battle of the sexes" until the Lord returns. Men and women strive to prove that theirs is the better gender. In relationships, individual men and women try to get the other to submit to their way.

But it's not just a battle of the sexes. We live in the world, and the world prefers selfishness over servanthood. The sinful world tells us it's better to be the king or boss so that you can tell other people what to do. It's better to be the parent than the child, because parents get to order kids around. It's better to be the teacher than the student, because the teacher controls the classroom and homework.

But here's the thing. When God places people into positions of authority, He places them to serve. In fact, God places us all in positions of service, whether we have authority over others or not. These are called "vocations." Right now, you may have the vocation of child, student, coworker, friend, church member, or the like. Luther wrote about this in his "Table of Duties" in the *Small Catechism*. Kings and rulers are reminded not to reign for their own gain, but to look out for the citizens entrusted to them. Likewise, bosses serve their employees by paying them a fair wage and providing a good work environment. Parents are called to care for and train their children thus serving them before they are even born. Teachers serve students by preparing them for the future with a solid education.

When people in authority use their authority for personal gain at the expense of others, they sin against God. They no longer act as servants, but as selfish sinners. Selfishness keeps on getting more selfish. A king who serves only himself will become a tyrant, whose subjects will no longer want to serve him. The same goes for a boss at work. A parent who fails to serve his child not only sets a poor example, but forces the child to look out for himself. By neglecting his child, he trains him to be selfish.

By the way, servanthood works between equals as well. When two people are simply friends, they ought to be servants to one another. That's what makes friendship work and grow.

Selfless Wisdom in a Selfish World

The Epistle of St. James sums up the battle of selfishness versus servanthood like this:

> *Who is wise and understanding among you? By his good conduct let him show his works in the meekness of wisdom. But if you have bitter jealousy and selfish ambition in your hearts, do*

not boast and be false to the truth. This is not the wisdom that comes down from above, but is earthly, unspiritual, demonic. For where jealousy and selfish ambition exist, there will be disorder and every vile practice. But the wisdom from above is first pure, then peaceable, gentle, open to reason, full of mercy and good fruits, impartial and sincere. And a harvest of righteousness is sown in peace by those who make peace. What causes quarrels and what causes fights among you? Is it not this, that your passions are at war within you? You desire and do not have, so you murder. You covet and cannot obtain, so you fight and quarrel. You do not have, because you do not ask. You ask and do not receive, because you ask wrongly, to spend it on your passions. You adulterous people! Do you not know that friendship with the world is enmity with God? Therefore whoever wishes to be a friend of the world makes himself an enemy of God. Or do you suppose it is to no purpose that the Scripture says, "He yearns jealously over the spirit that he has made to dwell in us"? But he gives more grace. Therefore it says, "God opposes the proud, but gives grace to the humble." JAMES 3:13–4:6

Those who have godly wisdom work in meekness, submitting their desires to the good of others.

This wisdom "from above is first pure, then peace-able, gentle, open to reason, full of mercy and good fruits, impartial and sincere" (James 3:17). These characteristics reflect a servant. For instance, those who are merciful care for others in need, and those who are willing to yield do not insist on their own way. Such wise serving fosters peace.

On the other hand, the sinful world's "wisdom" of "*selfish* ambition" is called "demonic" (James 3:14–15), not godly. Indeed, wars and fights (and failed relationships at all levels) result from selfish desires for pleasure, including lust and covetous-ness, murder, and adultery. All of these manifesta-tions result from selfish attempts to fulfill personal desires. Lust and covetousness cause one to desire things that God hasn't given, to gain at the expense of others. Murder seeks to improve one's life by ending somebody else's—that's about as far from servanthood as you can get! Such behaviors are contrary to God's Word, natural to the world, and most certainly *not* the characteristics of a servant. All of these temptations and sins dwell within our sinful nature.

But look! How does the Lord respond? He "gives more grace...to the humble" (James 4:6). See here your salvation. God *continues to serve* by bestowing forgiveness to all who will believe, for the sake of

His Son, Jesus, the suffering Servant who selflessly went to the cross in your place.

EXHORTATIONS TO HUSBANDS AND BRIDES

Anyway, back to marriage. Even though Adam and Eve fell into sin, the ideal of marriage remains. Husbands and wives are to serve one another. St. Paul makes this clear in his letter to the church at Ephesus.

> *Wives, submit to your own husbands, as to the Lord. For the husband is the head of the wife even as Christ is the head of the church, His body, and is Himself its Savior. Now as the church submits to Christ, so also wives should submit in everything to their husbands. Husbands, love your wives, as Christ loved the church and gave Himself up for her, that He might sanctify her, having cleansed her by the washing of water with the word, so that He might present the church to Himself in splendor, without spot or wrinkle or any such thing, that she might be holy and without blemish. In the same way husbands should love their wives as their own bodies. He who loves his wife loves himself. For no one ever hated his own flesh, but nourishes and cherishes it, just as Christ does the church, because we are members of His body.*

> *"Therefore a man shall leave his father and mother and hold fast to his wife, and the two shall become one flesh." This mystery is profound, and I am saying that it refers to Christ and the church. However, let each one of you love his wife as himself, and let the wife see that she respects her husband.* EPHESIANS 5:22–33

God's Word calls wives to submit to their husbands—to be servants. Through Paul's words, He goes on to explain that wives submit to their husbands *as the Church submits to Christ.* What does it mean that the Church submits to Christ? For example, every week we gather together for worship. As part of that worship we pray the Lord's Prayer. In the Lord's Prayer, we pray, "Thy will be done." In doing so, we announce that we desire to serve the Lord, not use the Lord to get our way. We pray that His will, not our selfish desires, be done. That's submission. Likewise, wives submit to their husbands in that they enter marriage to serve their husbands, not use their husbands in service to themselves.

Husbands are told to love their wives as *Christ loved the Church and gave Himself for her.* When Jesus became man, it was not to order people around. Instead, He said, "even as the Son of Man came not to be served but to serve, and to give His life as a ransom for many" (Matthew 20:28). He served all sinners to the point of dying in their place on the cross! Likewise, husbands are commanded to enter marriage to serve their wives, not enslave their wives in service to themselves.

This is the relationship that God sets up in marriage. Men and women have different God-given gifts and vocations, and they are to use them in service to one another. The husband is the head of the wife; upon him still rests the primary responsibility to feed his family with the Word of God, even as Adam was to do. But those who are given authority by God are always given authority to serve—not to dominate and control. And in each case, it is given to the husband and wife to serve each other. Serving one another is what God created us to do. "'And you shall love the Lord your God with all your heart and with all your soul and with all your mind and with all your strength.' The second is this: 'You shall love your neighbor as yourself.' There is no other commandment greater than these" (Mark 12:30–31).

But because of sin, we can't begin to carry out this simple command. That's why we dare not skip lightly past the references to our Lord Jesus Christ in Ephesians 5. In this passage, marriage illustrates the relationship between Christ and His bride—the

Church. Jesus Christ is the ultimate Servant. Where Adam blamed his bride Eve for his sin, Christ took on the blame of His bride and suffered death to save her. While sin condemned man to a life of selfishness, Jesus remained the Servant who selflessly died on the cross, and who now selflessly serves His people by forgiving their sins, by means of His Word and Sacraments. The Old Testament book of Hosea illustrates this poignantly. God calls the prophet, Hosea, to marry Gomer the prostitute. Even when Gomer returns to whoring and is sold into slavery, Hosea, the humiliated husband, is told by God to buy her back and redeem her from slavery. Likewise, even though the people of God continually sin and wander from His commands, the Lord—who redeemed them at the cross—still pursues them with His means of grace, restoring His bride to purity.

SUMMING UP

It should be no big surprise that two of the passages we just looked at (Genesis 2:18–24 and Ephesians 5:21–33), along with Matthew 19:4–6, are the appointed texts for the rite of marriage in the Lutheran Church. (See *Lutheran Worship Agenda*, p. 121; and *The Lutheran Agenda*, p. 42–43.) One order for marriage also includes Genesis 3:16–19 about the Fall into sin to proclaim "the cross which by reason of sin God hath laid upon this estate" (*The Lutheran Agenda*, p. 43). That's what I like about a Lutheran order of service for a wedding: Rather than wallow in a bunch of squishy sentiments that everyone knows won't last, the service tells what marriage is about, both the challenges and the joys. It describes what God wants marriage to be, and how sin seeks to mess it up. That's why when I meet with couples whose wedding I've been asked to conduct we examine these texts, along with the marriage vows. While we look at the Scripture texts I relentlessly hammer home the following points with these engaged couples:

1. God created people to be servants. Marriage is God's gift in which a husband and wife are called to be servants to each other for life.

Husband and wife are called to be servants to one another in *every* aspect of married life—chores, finances, sex, family, vacation, kids, jobs, and the list goes on. Servanthood strengthens marriage. I often tell couples, "Your marriage is on solid ground when your worst fight is, 'No honey, this time we're going to do it *your* way!'" This conversation often leads to the question about the word "obey" in the bride's vows. If the engaged couple are still servants to one another, then why does the bride vow to obey her husband, while the husband does not vow to obey his wife? In fact, many brides request that "obey" be deleted from the vows. But this request reflects a misunderstanding concerning the role of the husband and the terms of obedience. God entrusts the husband to provide spiritual life for his family. It is his responsibility to make sure that the Word is proclaimed to his wife [and children] through family devotions, church attendance, and the like. When the bride promises to obey her husband, she declares that she understands his obligation to make their house a godly home, and will support him in his efforts to do so. In reality, the bride's pledge to obey does not put her on the spot as much it does the groom. He must provide the Word for his family and lead them to honor and obey God's will.

2. The greatest enemy of marriage is selfishness.

Part of this conflict is environmental. As a little child, parents take care of you, and you get used to it. Very early you learn that by crying and complaining you can get others to give you food, clean clothes, a good burp, or whatever you think you need. As you grow up, your parents provide less direct care while giving you more responsibilities—but they still make sure that you have food, clothes, and a place to live. As a single adult, you learn to look after yourself. This move toward independence provides necessary training. But in most cases you still haven't been particularly trained to serve others. Then you get married. Suddenly you are called to put somebody else first—that takes some getting used to. Your well-trained sinful nature naturally wants you to be selfish—to use others as your servants.

When marriages develop trouble or divorce occurs, it is usually because one, or both parties involved, have become selfish and are no longer willing to serve the other. Scripture gives two legitimate reasons for divorce: adultery (Matthew 19:9) and abandonment (1 Corinthians 7:15). In the case of adultery, adulterers declare by their actions that they prefer their own happiness over faithfulness to their spouses. In the case of abandonment, those who leave declare that they prefer their own freedom over remaining in a relationship where they serve their families. Both acts are terribly selfish and destructive to a marriage.

On a daily basis, husband and wife fight the battle of selfishness versus servanthood. *Who will clean up the dishes? Change the diaper? With whose family will you spend Thanksgiving and Christmas? What should be done with the extra money? What should we do on Friday night?* With each question, the Old Adam tempts them to selfishly demand their own way. This is especially dangerous today because society views marriage as a selfish act. Couples should remain married so long as they both shall *love*, not so long as they both shall *live*. When a couple grows tired of life with one another, the world says that they should divorce and pursue happiness elsewhere.

The world does this with parenting, too. I still remember when my wife and I were expecting our first child. A woman counseled us, "Just make sure that your kids don't get in the way of your life." Though she thought it was good advice, the woman was cautioning us against servanthood in favor of selfishness. Kids pretty much *are* your life while they're growing up, since God entrusts you with their complete care and training. Be ready!

3. Because selfishness becomes a daily sin within marriage, confession and forgiveness need to be a daily part of marriage as well.

The life of the Christian is a life of repentance, confession and forgiveness. However, this can be especially hard in marriage when the couple understands that they are committed to each other for life. "I was wrong" is difficult to say because it does damage to your selfish pride; furthermore, there's the fear that your mate might selfishly store it up as ammunition for the next fight. "I forgive you" is equally hard to say because it means that you can't selfishly store up your mate's sin to use during the next fight. That's how the Old Adam wants it. But confession and absolution destroy the sins of self-ishness, and the forgiveness of Christ frees husband and wife to serve each other once again. In fact, confession and absolution serves as one of the greatest acts of service to one another, for it involves the denying of self, forgiving, and being forgiven for the sake of Jesus Christ.

4. In other words, servanthood is the key to marriage.

The world promotes the idea that good relation-ships just happen. Two people get together and it "just feels right." Technically speaking, the world is full of hooey. The "just feels right" idea might work for a little while, but not for long. Selfishness has a way of destroying that "right" feeling. Marriage—really any meaningful relationship—is built upon servanthood. The servanthood begins and ends with the service of Jesus Christ. Christ has redeemed you from sin and set you free to serve; it is with this Good News that He desires to bring couples into marriage. Because Christ has served them, they serve one another. When they fail, they confess their sins and receive forgiveness. While confession and absolution takes place in the home, it is also to take place in public worship. In the divine service, the couple hears together of Christ's forgiveness from their pastor, and they receive Jesus' body and blood for forgiveness, to strengthen them in faith—and thus in servanthood. It is called *divine service* for a reason: The divine Son of God is present, serving His people by forgiving their sins in His means of grace. He comes to serve you!

I'll add one more point, one that is not very popular and usually too late to talk about by the time the engaged couple is sitting in my office.

5. Both husband and wife need to share the same faith.

Specifically, they need to share the same faith in Jesus Christ. "Do not be unequally yoked with unbelievers. For what partnership has righteousness with lawlessness? Or what fellowship has light with darkness?" (2 Corinthians 6:14). Paul's words to the church at Corinth certainly have profound application to marriage. Indeed, I rarely hear it applied to anything *but* marriage. However, 2 Corinthians 6 is not about the relationship between husband and wife; it is a warning against listening to false teachers and false prophets so that the ministry of reconciliation—the preaching of the pure Gospel—can be maintained.

Because Christians face the growing fad of worshiping with those of other religions, it is important that this text receive its full recognition, not merely application to marriage alone. But regarding marriage, the need to share the Christian faith is important for several reasons:

First, a Christian enters into marriage as a servant.

Since the world does not teach servanthood, it's quite likely the unbelieving spouse will not see marriage as an opportunity for selfless service. They might see it as a 50–50 contract ("I'll do my part as long as you do yours"), but not as it relates to submission and serving. If the unbeliever has swallowed the teachings of the world, they'll think that marriage is a temporary relationship of convenience, to be preserved only as long as it feels fulfilling.

Second, the Christian works to solve differences on the basis of confession and forgiveness, because of Christ's redemption.

The unbeliever does not believe in Christ and won't work to resolve problems in the same way.

Third, it is extremely difficult for the believer to continue faithful church attendance while the unbeliever has no need or desire for worship. While it can work successfully, this subject remains a source of temptation and often friction.

Fourth, even if the believer remains a faithful church member, it is natural—as in the sinful nature—that the couple's children desire to follow the unbelieving parent's example and not attend worship.

So, should you marry someone within your own denomination, or is it good enough to simply marry a member of another Christian church? While marrying a Christian of another church body is better than marrying a non-Christian, these couples still encounter problems along the way. Essentially, "blended faith" couples have four choices:

> 1. One person can switch churches and join the other person's congregation.

> 2. Each spouse can attend separate services and be involved in two different church families, which doesn't do much for them being together.

> 3. They can alternate churches each week, which satisfies no one.

> 4. They can both just give up religion out of "love" for each other. While this might give them a happy life for a few decades, it can doom them for eternity.

One hopes that couples would go for option one,

with both attending a church where the Word is preached in its truth and purity and the Sacraments are administered according to the Word. However, this doesn't always happen, and the couple will never be quite as close as they could have been.

If the couple goes for options two, three, or maybe four, they may be satisfied—for a while—until children come along. At that point, one parent will want the baby baptized, while the other may oppose infant Baptism. This leads to lots of friction, which results in a child robbed of the blessings of Holy Baptism until an agreed-upon age. Children end up paying the price, living without the certainty of forgiveness and faith leading to eternal life!

Now, please understand where I'm coming from because I don't say these things lightly. I live in Idaho, where single Lutherans rank in population just above left-handed hamsters who skateboard—the dating pool is not exactly huge. I understand that what I've just said isn't welcome news. However, the Lord has a way of working beyond statistics and demographics to accomplish His will. I do know dating singles who accompanied their future spouse through adult confirmation class. Since they were already grounded in the Word, they insisted that their future mate also be confirmed in the same. At the same time, they were unwilling to continue the courtship if the other person did not accept the faith. One who does so must be willing to accept the potential, deeply painful, heartbreak that goes with the risk.

So . . . that's what I tell couples who are in my office, preparing for marriage. And while I tell them this stuff every time, I do so knowing two things:

First, I know that they're not listening to me. In most cases, they're so "in love" and have such high hopes for the future that I could recite poetry about my lawnmower and they wouldn't notice.

Second, even if couples see the enormous problem of selfishness that could devastate their marriage, by the time they're in my office they're going to count on "love" to get them through. They'll go ahead and get married no matter what I say.

That's why it's good to tell you all this now, when marriage is still a ways away and your head remains somewhat clear. That's also why, when you're dating, it's good for you to think about these things and see how they apply even when you're just going out for a pizza on a Friday night.

know thyself

chapter

two

chapter two

This is now. And, for now, it's just you.

Here are a few things that are true about you now, between the ages of 13 and 20.

If you are between the ages of 13 and 20, you are currently in a process called differentiation: You're becoming more and more independent. Think of it this way: When you were younger, you had no independence. Your parents governed everything you did because you were "just a little kid." When you got to kindergarten or so, you got a *little* more inde-

pendence; you were under the close supervision of a
teacher, but not your parents. (By the way, this step
alone was really tough for many of your folks.) A
little bit older, and you got to go on a sleepover to a
friend's house, then maybe a camping trip with a
group.

If you're already sixteen, you might have a dri-
ver's license and don't even need mom or dad to
chauffeur you around anymore: You've become even
more independent. From your viewpoint, that's
probably pretty cool. Even though you're more
independent, sometimes you dislike that your parents are still giving you orders. From your parents'
viewpoint, they've been trying hard for a decade
and a half to prepare you to be an adult, and they're
worried that they haven't had enough time. This is
why the teenage years can be so combative, silent, or
perhaps just tense in a household. The teenager is
saying, "I want to get going," and the parents are
saying, "Not so fast." To make life a lot more com-
plicated, at the same time, your body is changing
more radically than it ever will again.

During your teenage years you will be excited
about and relish the new freedoms and independence that you're getting. At the same time you will
do some really stupid things with that newfound
freedom and independence. Make no mistake, the

teenage years are a tough transition—mentally, physically, and emotionally. It's a cauldron of bubbling changes that can leave you really confused, embarrassed, and unsure of yourself. That's why I have two distinct emotions about high school. On the one hand, I enjoyed most of it. On the other hand, I never want to go through it again.

To top it all off this may well be the time that you start dating. Once upon a time you couldn't sit up without help . . . now you're going out with a member of the opposite sex. This process can be especially disconcerting for your parents. It is also another step in differentiating. By dating, you acknowledge that you're becoming an adult, and that you're responsible and mature enough to spend unsupervised time with members of the opposite sex. In other words, dating is a milestone in life, one that signals future relationships lie ahead that will only get more serious, and may lead to marriage.

All of this may seem light years away from going out for a burger and a movie. In reality, if you're sixteen years old, you'll be a legal adult in less than two years; even though for now, you still need your parents to sign permission slips. If you are 16 years old, statistically speaking you'll probably be married ten years from now. The clock is running. The times they are a-changing.

As a teenager a lot is happening fast. But on top of all those changes, let's add a couple more truths.

YOU'RE SINFUL. This means that you are going to make some bad decisions along the way—sometimes with complete ignorance, sometimes with plenty of planning and malice. The world calls this part of growing up. While it's true, it's no excuse. Before God, it's sin. As a sinner you deal daily with other sinners. Your sinful nature only motivates you toward selfishness. Your sinful self wants only what pleases itself; you want others to serve you.

YOU'RE FORGIVEN. Jesus Christ went to the cross and died for your sins. While this has always been true, it may be a special comfort during these years of transition. Some of the mistakes you make may be very public and very mortifying—where you wonder if you can ever show your face again. They may be shameful enough so that you wonder if you can forgive yourself. But be confident of this:

45

No matter what your conscience is screaming, Jesus forgives you. Confess your sins, hear His absolution and know that the Lord, the suffering Servant, died for you to take away your sin. By His grace, you are set free. As a forgiven saint, you are set free to serve others—not build yourself up selfishly at their expense.

So here you are. You're a saint and a sinner, somewhere between child and adult, your body changing rapidly whether you're ready or not, trying to honor your parents even while you're trying to become independent of them. If you wonder why you feel like a conflicted mess sometimes, now you know.

This also means that, right now, you are caught in a battle between selfishness and servanthood. Your old sinful nature wants to draw attention to yourself, one way or another, while the saint in you wants to act and be a servant to others. That constant internal battle produces interesting results in the life of the Christian teen. For instance:

✱ Beauty is a gift from God. While there's nothing wrong with wanting to look your best as your body matures, there's a temptation to wear clothes that draw attention to the parts that look different than they did when you were a kid, if you know what I mean. That's vanity, a self-serving desire to be envied.

✱ There are a lot of people on television who talk, act, and dress to draw attention to themselves and their sexuality. Television producers figure that if they can get half-naked people to do and say crass things on television, people will watch. Like cows staring at a fence post, or folks who slow down to gawk at a wreck on the highway, they can't tear themselves away from the scene. The producers are right—but are they right about *you*? The temptation exists to leave the show on and fill your mind with this garbage. Using other people's bodies and behavior to gratify your own imagination is selfishness and lust. You fill your mind with impure stuff in disobedience to God's command.

✱ There's nothing wrong with the desire to be liked, even popular. But, all too often, part of being popular means shutting out those who aren't popular—people who could use a little kindness and help.

✱ The desire to excel is good. The desire to excel at the expense of others is not. It's easy to make yourself feel better by making others feel bad.

✷ The goal of producing good grades is an admirable one. However, when you don't quite earn the grade you want, there's the temptation to cut corners and cheat in order to make yourself look better than you are. It's amazing what your selfish pride can talk you into sometimes.

✷ Because of differentiation, you're learning to make independent decisions. Some of this is good. You need to become independent. After all, your mother does not want you to call her and ask which socks to wear when you're forty years old. However, when you disobey your parents, you have selfishly said that you'd rather serve yourself than keep the Fourth Commandment and honor them.

In every case, at every age, this is true: When you go against God's Word, one of the sins at work is selfishness: "I want what I want, not what God wants."

You live in a world of "do," "don't," and "doesn't matter." There are some things that the Bible says are just plain sin, some things in life the Bible commands—see the Ten Commandments (Exodus 20:1–17) for details. There are also a lot of things in life that the Bible doesn't forbid or command, and these things you can do with common sense in Christian freedom.

This is true in dating, too. Because dating often means that you're away from parents and authority figures, it presents opportunities for all sorts of things that are sinful, breaking God's Law and state law, such as underage drinking, illegal drug use, and transporting endangered reptiles across state lines. It also includes too much physical affection and premarital sex.

Dating also provides opportunities for all sorts of fun things: let's say mini golf, for example. Now you're probably thinking, "Can there be anything more harmless than mini golf?" Let me tell you, and judge for yourself: I took a date mini golfing once. This date was so successful that she didn't speak to me for four months, and then only to say that she didn't want to go out again. Broke my heart. Golf at your own risk, and don't say I didn't warn you.

At the same time don't be fooled into thinking that a "fun" date is only one that pushes the edge of right and wrong. People define "fun" differently. In these parts, a "fun" thing to do is to get a bunch of underage friends together with a case of beer, drive out into the desert, sit on hard rocks and drink until you throw up. These super-secret places are carefully mapped out and patrolled by local law enforcement agencies, who show up, hand you a cell phone and tell you to call your parents and tell them that you're in custody for driving out into the desert, sitting on hard rocks and drinking beer underage until you throw up. Yeah. Fun.

Now, in the world of do, don't and doesn't matter, it can get pretty murky. Something can be perfectly fine and innocent, but taken another step or two, it gets sinful. Wearing attractive clothing is fine; wearing clothes that provoke lewd attention to your body is not. Physical affection in the form of holding hands is probably okay, but one step of physical affection will lead to another, and some of those steps are wrong until marriage. The Bible doesn't forbid dancing, but a rave with drugs or moves that simulate sex acts are not the purity that the Lord has called you to. Dinner and conversation can be a great date—unless the conversation is all gossip about other people. Mini golf turns ugly about the time you start using your putter to destroy the windmill after it's humiliated you. Again. Stupid windmill.

When does a "doesn't matter" turn into a "don't"? Common sense—a vastly underrated gift from God—will tell you a lot. Also, the better you know God's Word, the more sensitive you'll be to right and wrong. A great question you can use to measure this is: "Would I be ashamed if my parents found out about this?" Your parents are, after all, called by God to be your parents, appointed by Him to raise you up right. There's a reason why the same sin makes you ashamed before God and your folks; when things are running the way the Lord desires, they're teamed up with Him to do what's best for you.

All of this has to do with how you date. When you go out with someone, both the selfish sinner and the serving saint come along. You'll have the opportunity to do moral things, immoral things, legal things, and illegal things. The dilemmas arise, and dating can be a selfish thing. For instance . . .

> A girl goes out with a guy because he has lots of money and spends it on her.

> A guy goes out with a girl because she's popular, and it makes him look good.

> One goes out with another because, well, they really don't like the other, but at least it's a date.

> A couple goes out because one likes to get physical fast, and the other feels important because of the physical affection. Both are selfish desires.

Do you think this changes and gets easier when you're an adult? Think again! Grown-ups face the same temptations, but the consequences only get bigger. People will marry to get money or popularity or status or power. They may marry someone incompatible only because they don't want to be alone. Many will get married because they're already having sex and figure that's a good enough foundation for a lifetime of commitment. But marriage is about servanthood. Marriage that begins as a selfish act is likely to lead to disaster. Dating that's based on selfishness won't be much better.

the dating/marriage connection

chapter
three

chapter three

I keep mentioning marriage because, like it or not, marriage and dating are connected.

You may not see a huge bridge between a school dance and exchanging wedding vows, but the connection is greater than you think. In fact, it has often and wisely been said that you should never date anyone that you couldn't marry. That may sound crazy, but consider the following:

Chances are pretty remote that you will marry

the only person you ever date; it happens, but not often. However, chances are about 100% that, if you marry, you will marry someone whom you've dated. Why would you marry someone that you haven't dated? Why would they marry you?

Dating usually starts out around the age of 16 years old, about halfway through high school, although that age will—and should—vary. Statistics say that you will probably be married by the age of 25. Between now and then, you will go from a casual "burger and a movie" date to serious courtship and looking for a mate for life. When will you make that transition? Seriously, I'm asking: *When do you plan to go from casual to serious dating?* If you're sixteen, that means you've got about two years of high school left. After that, four years of college. After that, you have three years until you're 25; and the law of averages says that by then you're probably married. So when do you make the transition? When does dating become serious?

Chances are that you will never consciously make the transition from casual dating to serious courtship. You can't predict when "the one" will appear in your life. It's quite common that you'll develop a deep attraction to someone you've known casually for a while. This is largely beyond your control. You do not know when this will happen.

It's a good habit to have good habits from the start. If you're in sports or play video games, you know this to be true. Skills for any given task require training and repetition to develop good habits. If you practice poor discipline throughout your training regimen, you won't be prepared when the big game comes along. The same holds true in all aspects of life. Self-discipline and good habits lead to success, more often than not. Get into the habit of dating quality people—people with whom you could spend your life. This is important on two counts. As mentioned before, you don't know when you'll meet your future mate. If you get in the habit of dating the wrong people, you'll probably stay in the habit of dating the wrong people. Not only that, but understand that, as a Christian, you are called upon to serve others. To be a quality companion is to be a servant. To have a quality companion is to be with someone who also knows the importance of serving. Get in the habit of looking for one now.

While there's a lot of casual dating that has no intention of leading to marriage, the possibility is always lurking that it will. That's why you want to set your standards high and keep this all in the back of your mind from the very beginning.

crushes
and
compatibility

chapter

four

chapter four

Who are you going to date?

That's up to you, not me. But remember that at least this much is true about whoever it is. Thanks to that old sinful nature, they are also going to struggle with selfishness versus servanthood.

Many people choose whom they'd like to date based upon emotions. You know the feeling—you meet someone that you can't stop thinking about, who takes your breath away. Every time you see the person, your heart skips a beat, violins play, and the sun seems to shine more brightly while the birds sing even chirpier songs. Your cheerfulness annoys everyone around you. You know you can't live without that one special person. You spend endless hours in class doodling the person's name on a piece of paper. Then some cranky chemistry teacher plucks it off your desk during a lecture and reads it to the class. And you're just mortified and scarred for life and start to hate science and so you drop the whole idea of becoming a doctor and pretty soon you're sitting at your desk writing books on dating and thinking about how you could have discovered the cure for some disease and . . . uh . . . and . . .

Heh, heh. Uh, just kidding! Phew!

Anyway, the technical term for this kind of a crush is "infatuation," which has to be one of the ugliest sounding words in the English language. It doesn't help that it appears in the dictionary right between "infarction" and "infection." Alas, I digress again. An infatuation is a purely emotional affection for someone, and therein lies the problem.

Don't get me wrong. I like emotions. They're a gift from God. But emotions are difficult to control since they are largely governed by forces beyond your control. A lot of it has to do with your energy level. You probably already know that you're happier to see your family in the morning when you've had a good night's sleep than if you're dog-tired. In the same way you'll react to the same people differently depending on how much energy you've got. You don't want to base a relationship on something like, "I'll like you as long as I'm well-rested and in a good mood." Furthermore, emotions like extremes: When you've got a crush on someone, every little smile convinces you that you're made for each other, and every frown panics you that it's all falling apart—whatever "it" may be.

As helpful as emotions are, don't make them the sole reason for doing things, especially not dating. You need to do the right thing no matter how you feel. Along the way, examine emotions as results of what you've done or symptoms of what's going on. While I don't have complete statistics on emotions and dating, the primary reason many couples get married is that they "feel love" for each other. Marriage experts tell us that these "feeling" emotions are capable of sustaining a marriage—for *maybe* two years. Hey, that leaves you with a just few *decades* with nothing to go on. This, by the way, is why pastors get so many troubled couples in their office who have been married for three or four years. The feelings can't sustain the marriage anymore.

Furthermore, a crush can be a very selfish thing. "He has to care about *me* because *I* care so much about him!" There's not much of a servant attitude in that statement. A good relationship is based on servant principles. For example, "I'm going to do my best to put you first today, whether I feel like it or not." Crushes happen, and they can be fun for a while. But don't take them too seriously, or else they can really beat you up. It's called a "crush" for a reason; it describes what happens to you when you end one.

Now, we've already stated that any relationship involves a battle of selfishness versus servanthood, in which both individuals need to give up their personal preferences in service to the other. In other words, in a perfect world, any man and woman could get together and—by giving up what doesn't serve the other—have a successful, meaningful, life-long relationship.

However, you do not live in a perfect world. You live in a sinful world where the default setting for each person is "I want *my* way." This is why compatibility, having things in common, is so important. It's simple. Whenever two people have something in common, they don't have to struggle with which one has to give up what they like. Instead, they can go about serving each other in something they both agree upon. When two people have little in common, then they'll always be fighting about who gives up their preference in favor of the other.

For instance, you may know a couple where she likes to go to the mall and he likes to watch sports. They both hate what the other one likes to do. Every time they get together, one of them has to sacrifice what they like and do what they hate. This is not a good basis for a relationship. A couple with similar interests and beliefs is likely to last a whole lot longer.

Compatibility isn't just about doing things. It's about religion, morality, work, school, how much time to spend together and alone, and eventually where to live and how many children to have. Even if the two of you are amazingly compatible, you're still sinful and you're still going to have selfish arguments about doing things your way. If you have very little in common, it means you're going to argue a whole lot more because you have more issues that differ.

So, what's important to note as you begin dating? Use dating as an opportunity to discover whether or not you're compatible with someone. Learn how much you're willing to sacrifice, and what things you're neither willing to sacrifice nor compromise on. Why is this important? When you discover relationships that are just too incompatible while dating, you can break it off and walk away. While it's not pleasant, it's often the right thing to do. Once married, however, you've vowed "'Til death do us part." This promise made before God commits you to staying and serving—even when it becomes difficult. The old proverb teaches a good lesson, "When dating, look at your date with both eyes wide open. When you get married, close one eye."

While selfishness destroys compatibility, servanthood strengthens it. The more two people put each other first, the deeper the love grows. I recall one woman's advice to girls, "For a husband, find someone who is easy to submit to." In other words, look for someone whom you can serve, and who understands the importance of servanthood. Watch how your date treats other people (ushers, coworkers, classmates, waitresses, and others). Once the romance dies down, that's how they'll be treating you.

When dating someone, remember the adage "what you see is what you get." Many young people continue in a relationship secretly thinking, "I'll change him later on." I know a gentleman who just celebrated his 50th wedding anniversary. He once shared with me, "When a woman gets married, she wants to change the man. When a man gets married, he wants to keep the woman exactly the same." There's great wisdom in his statement, but rarely does either hope work out. While it may be possible, don't count on it. Someone who talks a lot will always talk a lot. Someone who always runs late will seldom ever be on time. How would you like it if your date was secretly saying, "I'm going to change you later on"? The reality is, when you're dating, what you see is probably better than normal, since most people naturally try to look and behave their best to make a good impression on their date.

No couple is perfectly compatible. Even if they have similar interests, they also have that old sinful, selfish nature inside. This means that servanthood will not always be easy and compromise is a must. It also means that confession and forgiveness must be part of the relationship. Both individuals have weaknesses that need to be compensated for. Each has strengths that will strengthen the other. Each will compromise in service to the other. This is why each year in November, many men make the long-range calculation and sit through *The Sound of Music* in hopes of watching the Super Bowl undisturbed. (If you don't think that was a funny line, your dad will.)

Some people say that a couple that never fights does not have a healthy relationship. To a certain extent that makes sense. Why? Because couples are bound to disagree at times. If they never fight, it means that one person is always giving in while the other is always winning. As odd as it may seem, it's a good thing when a couple has at least one big fight before they get married. More than a few battles will be fought after they're husband and wife, so it's good for them to know how they'll act and react before they are married.

Most importantly a couple's compatibility can't exclude the Lord. A couple may have a great relationship with one another yet completely deny the Savior's mercy for a lifetime. Their mutual selfishness that rejects the Lord's mercy includes the Lord's sacrifice for their sin. While their relationship may go on for years, they may well encourage each other right into eternal judgment. Serving one another for the sake of getting along can never mean disobeying God.

the law and the gospel of getting dumped

chapter five

chapter five

Earlier we mentioned that you will likely not marry the only person you ever date.

In other words, you will date a few—in some cases more than a few—other people before you meet the one you marry. This means that along the way you *will* be involved in a relationship that ends. You need to be prepared for the reality that you will either dump someone, be dumped by someone, or both.

Experts at getting dumped concur that it really, really stinks.

There's a ton of emotion that accompanies ending a relationship that makes it nearly impossible to think objectively, so it's good to work it through beforehand. Why do relationships end? There can be a lot of reasons, but the fundamental truth is pretty simple. It takes *two* people to make a relationship work, but it only takes *one* to destroy it.

Now it should come as no big surprise here, but there's usually a lot of selfishness involved—by one or both individuals—when a relationship ends. The relationship might fall apart because one individual wants to pursue something, or even someone, on his or her own. Sometimes the pairing might end because one person selfishly demanded too much time and attention from the other. Whatever the reason, relationships end.

If you're the one being dumped, it hurts. Bad! Most likely you've been working very hard to make the other person accept you, to make the relationship work, yet they've chosen to reject you. That rejection usually makes the "dumpee" feel pretty worthless. As if that isn't enough trouble, there's an additional danger here. When you're attracted to someone, you're tempted to base your self-worth on what that person thinks about you. If they like you,

you must be worth something. If they don't, you must be worthless. This feeling of worthlessness is more likely to happen when you are "in love." Because love causes such strong emotions, it often leads to tunnel vision as you focus on the one you're attracted to. Because of the narrow space you're operating in, the whole world seems to be falling apart when you get dumped.

In the grand scheme of things, what are you worth?

Before God, you're worth the sacrificial death of His only-begotten Son on the cross. In other words, you're priceless! "But you are a chosen people, a royal priesthood, a holy nation, a people belonging to God, that you may declare the praises of Him who called you out of darkness into His wonderful light" (1 Peter 2:9).

So here's the Law: If you decide your worth based upon what another sinful human being says about you, you are saying that a sinful human being's opinion about you overrides God's declaration about you. You're saying that the one who dumped you has a greater say than God does. This is a dangerous sin. It's also, by the way, a very common sin for people of all ages.

Here's the Gospel: The Lord won't dump you. He's made you a part of His Church—His Bride, and He's done so by suffering and dying in your place. You have a faithful Bridegroom who has already given you the gift of eternal life. "For I am sure that neither death nor life, nor angels nor rulers, nor things present nor things to come, nor powers, nor height nor depth, nor anything else in all creation, will be able to separate us from the love of God in Christ Jesus our Lord" (Romans 8:38–39). He forgives you for the times that you base your value on the opinions of others instead of His Word about you.

All this said, getting dumped still really, really stinks. You're going to feel low for a while. But time heals all wounds (*and wounds all heels, which may give you some satisfaction given some of the jerks out there*). After a while, the opinion of that one person isn't going to hurt so much. And throughout the time in between, the Lord's love and favor for you doesn't change. It may *feel* as if God has taken the day off from loving you, but from His Word you know better. He's working all things for your good—"And we know that for those who love God all things work together for good, for those who are called according to His purpose" (Romans 8:28). And where you sometimes can't see past the disappointment of today, the Lord is shaping the future for your benefit—"For I know the plans I have for you, declares the LORD, plans for wholeness and not for evil, to give you a future and a hope" (Jeremiah 29:11).

Can you still be friends after the dating relationship ends? It all depends on how long you've been dating. The longer you were together, the longer the time until you can be friends again. Until then, I hate to say, you can't "just be friends." Here's why: After a break-up, the dumpee still wants to be more than friends while the dumper wants to be less than friends. One person is trying to pursue, one is trying to get away. The more one person insists on still being close, the more the other is going to resist. It's going to take some time, maybe a lot of time, before the wound heals. Even then, it won't ever be quite the same.

Now, since dumping involves two people, at some point in time you may well be the dumper instead of the dumpee. If that's the case, I offer two quick observations. First, ending a dating relationship is not necessarily a bad thing. There are some really creepy people out there. You may find yourself dating someone who is really not compatible with you, or who wants you to compromise your character or morals, and lead you into sin. One of the purposes of dating is to find out more about the other person. When you date, you don't vow to date "'Til death do us part." Dating either ends with marriage, or else dating ends with the end of the relationship. Sometimes, ending the relationship becomes a very good and smart thing to do.

The second point is this: If you're the one who has to end a relationship, remember what I said about getting dumped before. The person you're talking to may have based their self-worth on your opinion. Be kind and be honest, but don't give false hope. If you can, try to tell the person that their worth depends on Jesus, not on you. Finally—be realistic—know that they'll think it all really, really stinks; it's hard to accept and it's going to hurt. And it's going to be a long time—if ever—before you're friends again.

number 4 still applies

chapter six

chapter six

My high school had an unwritten rule about dating.

Before a guy could take a girl out on a date, he had to ask her father's permission first.

Speaking for the rest of the guys, we really hated that rule. It was bad enough summoning up the courage to ask a girl on a date. It was sheer torture calling her father. Some girls didn't like this rule. A lot of them did because it provided some nice cover—if some loser was after them, then the father could be the one to tell him to take a hike. Now that

I'm a dad, my outlook has changed. Even though I have no daughters, the whole idea doesn't seem that bad after all. Instead, I have two sons, and I want to make sure that they understand the relationship between parents and their children who are going out. After all, it's only 27 more years until my eight-year-old will be allowed to date. At least, if this overprotective father gets his way.

"Honor your father and your mother." That's the Fourth Commandment, and it applies to you. Unless you're already a legal adult, you are living under the authority of a parent, two parents, or some other legal guardian who is acting as a parent toward you. (Even when you're grown up, it still applies.) For the sake of space, I'll refer to all of these arrangements generically as "parents." Earlier in this book we listed a few universal truths about you; now, we need to list a few universal truths about you and your parents.

First, parents are God's instruments for your good. "Children, obey your parents in the Lord, for this is right. 'Honor your father and mother' (this is the first commandment with a promise), 'that it may go well with you and that you may live long in the land.'" (Ephesians 6:1–3). That's what the Bible says. You'll also find fitting texts in the "Table of Duties" in Luther's Small Catechism. Note several things: Before your parents ever tell you to obey them, God has told you to obey them. You're supposed to honor your parents, because if they are "in the Lord," they are instructing you carefully in right and wrong. If you do what they tell you, you should stay out of trouble and live long on the earth. Disobey them, and trouble is bound to result. The world likes to erode parental authority by teaching that you happen to have the parents you have because his sperm got to her egg, and it's all an accidental arrangement. You're just a coincidence, nothing more. God says differently: Your parents are your parents because God made them your parents for your good.

Also, parents are called to be godly examples and teachers. With authority comes responsibility, and the Bible calls upon parents to act accordingly. "Fathers, do not provoke your children to anger, but bring them up in the discipline and instruction of the Lord" (Ephesians 6:4). A parent can provoke a child to wrath by being harsh and cruel, thus failing to serve the child with compassion and kindness. On the other hand, a parent can provoke a child to wrath by failing to train and discipline; a child who receives little attention from his parents will likely to get into trouble and resent his or her parents for their neglect.

Third, parents are servants. Remember what we said before? When God places people into positions of authority, He gives them authority to serve. There are few things in life that demand more service than a newborn child, who can't do anything for himself. Parents provide this service seven days a week, 24 hours a day, often with little thanks. As children grow older, parents give them more tasks to perform so that they learn the importance of responsibility and service. Throughout their lives, parents continue to serve their children.

Fourth, parents aren't perfect; they're sinful, too. Parents get sinfully angry, frustrated, and impatient just like anybody else. Hopefully, this leads them to attend worship often, so that they can hear again the message of God's forgiveness for them. Prayerfully they are also training you in the importance of regular worship, since now you are in the process of picking up all of their good (or bad) habits. And hopefully, your parents ask your forgiveness when they've sinned against you. The point is—it's not fair or right to expect your parents to be perfect—and it's not right to ignore what they tell you because they're not perfect. Adam and Eve brought sin into the world long before the Lord commanded you to honor your father and mother.

Finally, your parents want what's best for you.

This is why they teach you manners and morals and make sure you get your homework done. They may even be making you read this for the same reason. It may not seem like it, but your parents are doing their best to make sure you turn out even better than they did. Sadly, this isn't a universal truth. There are some parents who are so much in bondage to sin that they have lost the basic decency to care even for their own children. In most cases, though, no father or mother starts out saying, "I sure hope that, by neglect and bad example, we can ruin our kids and their future."

Having considered these five points concerning your parents, I offer the following suggestions for dealing with parents when it comes to teenage years and dating.

First, your parents are great resources for teaching and understanding right and wrong. Face it, they've lived a lot longer than you. They've seen what bad decisions can cause. In some cases, they've seen friends get hurt for doing the wrong thing. In other cases, they've done the wrong thing and have had to pay the consequences themselves. Along with their understanding of God's Word, your parents have these experiences in mind when they're taking care of you.

So keep a couple of things in mind for yourself:

✱ **First, your parents will seem very restrictive at times because (a) you're in the process of differentiating and want to do new things, and (b) your parents know what "new things" can lead to.** As restrictive as your parents rules may seem, part of the reason for conflict between you and your parents is that you're driven to be a bit too independent during these years. Also, one of the lowest things that you can ever do is throw a parent's sin back in their face. For example, "You say I can't, but you did that when you were my age!" It's a cheap shot that really accomplishes nothing, other than to show that you're not the sharpest tool in the shed. Think about it: If your mom or dad made a stupid mistake and suffered for it, do you think that they want you to do the same? Or would they do everything they could to try to prevent you from doing the same stupid thing?

✱ **Second, your parents are far more objective than you are in any given situation.** We mentioned earlier that there are a ton of emotions swirling around when it comes to dating and crushes and the like. You can tell when your friend is dating a loser, even if they're oblivious. That's because they're infatuated with said loser, and you're not. Likewise, you may be all googly-eyed for someone because you don't see his or her faults, which would be obvious to someone more impartial. Your parents will not suffer from your tunnel vision, and by now they probably have developed some very good instincts. If they have reservations about the person you're dating, there's probably a very good reason for it. You might like to think they have no reason for their opinion, but they most likely have life experiences that influence their opinion. By the way, your parents retain their objectivity and instincts when you're an adult and will have their antennae trained at any special friend or fiancé that you bring their way. Although meeting the parents is an intimidating thing, your parents provide an excellent resource toward understanding what's best for you.

✱ Third, like it or not, you currently have the vocation of son or daughter. This is your God-given calling. With it comes the responsibility of serving your parents by giving them obedience and honor. How important is this? It's explicitly one of the Ten Commandments. "Honor your father and your mother, that your days may be long in the land that the LORD your God is giving you" (Exodus 20:12). To ignore your parents, fight with them, shut them out or undermine them is a selfish act of sin. This can be an active rebellion or something far more passive. Sadly we all fall into this sin pretty easily. As a teen I pretty much simply stopped speaking to my parents for a few years, which made dinner each evening a bit uncomfortable. It's a wonder they didn't send me to mime reform school. When you do fall into this sin of disrespect, it's time to confess it to your parents, remembering that the Lord has died for all of these sins, too.

✳ Fourth, given what we've just said, it only makes sense to work with your parents, not against them or behind their backs. As difficult as it may be for both you and them, before dating begins, get some basic ground rules down so that everyone knows what's expected later on. Who will you date? What sorts of activities are acceptable and unacceptable on dates? What time do you have to be home? Who's paying for gas? The more you get sorted out now, the less chance of misunderstanding later.

✳ Guess what? That person you're considering dating has parents too! Just as you pick up habits— both good and bad—from your parents, they will do the same from theirs. You can usually learn a lot about someone you date by talking to his or her folks. Who knows, you may get a preview of what he or she will be like twenty years down the road. By contrast, some people may be the polar opposite of his or her parents, and after meeting his or her parents you may well begin to understand why.

✱ Finally, there's one more good reason to get to know your significant other's parents. The Fourth Commandment doesn't fade away when you grow up. Should you get married, it extends to your in-laws, too.

the law and
the gospel of
physical affection

chapter
seven

Before we talk about sex, let's start out with the following dialogue.

Meet Robert and Sally, smitten with love. I'll let you imagine the violin music or whatever else you want to provide to enhance the drama that follows.

> **HIM:** Sally, we've been going out for a while now, and I want you to have this ring as an expression of my love and devotion to you.

HER: Oh, Robert! What a special gift! I'll bet it's beautiful! (Opens box) Hmmm . . . It's nice, but it looks like there used to be six little diamonds and one big one. They seem to be missing.

HIM: Well, yeah. When Sue gave it back to me, all the diamonds were gone.

HER: Sue? Who's Sue?

HIM: My ex-girlfriend. I thought we really had something there, so I gave her the ring. And later on, she gave it back.

HER: Well, I suppose that a slightly used ring can still be special. Too bad she took all the diamonds.

HIM: Actually, no. She took the six little ones. The big one was already gone.

HER: Oh. And that's because . . . ?

HIM: That's because Angela took the big diamond.

HER: Of course. And who, pray tell, is Angela?

HIM: She was my girlfriend before Sue. She and I got along great, so I gave her the ring before I gave it to Sue. When she gave it back, she kept the big diamond.

HER: This ring has quite a history.

HIM: Well, yeah. But I think it's still pretty special, and I want you to have it.

HER: It's kind of flattened on one side, like somebody gave it back to you by throwing it at you.

HIM: Um . . . yes, that's true. It hit the brick wall behind me when I ducked.

HER: Wow. Who threw it—Sue or Angela?

HIM: Uh, actually it was Melanie.

HER: Melanie. She was . . . ?

HIM: She was a girl I used to hang out with after Sue and Angela. We didn't know each other that well. But one night after a party, I gave it to her. The next morning, though, when she saw the diamonds were missing, she gave it back to me.

HER: Threw it back at you.

HIM: Whatever. The point is that it's still my ring. I still think it's pretty special, and I want you to have it because I think you're pretty special.

HER: Special? You mean a seriously damaged ring that you've given to three other girls?

HIM: Um, four, actually.

HER: Four?!

HIM: Well, there was Nancy, too.

HER: I stand corrected. This seriously damaged ring is so "special" that you've already given it to four other girls?

HIM: Well, yes.

HER: Robert?

HIM: Yes?

HER: You may think it's still special. But it's really not very special at all anymore. I suppose that I'm really not all that special to you either since all you can give me is a used, beaten-up ring.

HIM: It's all I have to give.

HER: Even so. It may be all you have to give, but it's just not that special anymore, and it never will be again.

As silly as this little scenario seems, the way this young man treats his "special" ring is exactly the same way that some young people treat God's plan concerning sex.

The Lord gives the gifts of sex and marriage, and He declares that sex and marriage go together. If marriage involves servanthood, this means that sex and servanthood go together. To those of you reading this book this concept may sound really, really strange. But within the context of marriage, sex becomes a means by which a husband and wife care for one another. Their faithfulness to each other over the years also strengthens and enriches their marriage.

Sex serves as a powerful part of marriage with physical, mental, and emotional components. The intimacy and faithfulness involved in a sexual relationship helps create an indescribable bond between husband and wife. This is why infidelity becomes so destructive to marriage—it shatters the bond at so many levels.

Sex was designed as God's means of procreation (producing children), and procreation definitely involves servanthood! In other words, sex becomes the means by which life is brought into the world for service. When a husband and wife conceive a child, the opportunities for servanthood grow. The mother-to-be cares for the child for nine months before birth, while the father-to-be tries to make his wife's life easier during this stressful time. When children are born, the parents care for their child's needs throughout their formative years. As adults, grown children serve God, man, and creation through their various vocations. "And God said to them, 'Be fruitful and multiply and fill the earth and subdue it and have dominion over the fish of the sea and over the birds of the heavens and over every living thing that moves on the earth'" (Genesis 1:28). The "fruitful and multiply" part leads to the service of filling the earth, subduing it, and having dominion over it. While some have confused what these words mean, they are servant words since positions of leadership are actually positions of service to those being led.

Sex and servanthood go together. God gave sex as a means of serving between husband and wife, who in turn serve the creation by producing more servants. Sex is a precious gift: The Lord creates you with the ability to bring life into the world. Think about that! A gift so precious—and so powerful—to be cherished and used according to the Word of the Giver.

Now, the enemy of servanthood is selfishness; therefore, the enemy of sex is selfishness, as well. But strip away everything the world says, and this is true. In the world's plan, sex becomes a tool and a matter of selfishness. This is how the world approaches sex—not as a way of serving, but as an act of selfishness. In other words, the world teaches that you are a sexual creature, and that you should use sex in whatever way gratifies *you*.

So what does this mean for you? Here's one way

it plays out in high school: A few weeks before prom, a senior guy starts dating a freshman girl. He flatters her with all sorts of attention and asks her to be his prom date. The girl, pleased with the interest from an older guy, quickly develops a huge crush on him. Prom night comes along and after the dance, they're all alone. The guy tells the girl that he'd like to make love to her—that if she truly loves him, she'll have sex with him. The girl may have doubts, but on second thought, she's got a huge crush on the guy and doesn't want to lose him, so she consents. So, which one is being selfish? Both of them! The guy wants to have sex, and he's essentially purchased it through flattery and gifts. The girl wants to keep his attention, and she's willing to use sex to do so. He's seeking physical enjoyment and she's seeking emotional gratification, but both are engaged in sex in order to make themselves happy.

Of course, a relationship built upon such selfishness is doomed to fail. Having gotten what he wanted, chances are good that he'll dump her the next day. She'll become a locker-room boast of his conquest so that he can feed his selfish pride at her expense. In doing so, he's training himself to treat women as objects for his pleasure, and thus training himself not to be a servant and never to have a solid marriage. Used and spurned, with her pride shattered, depression likely follows for the girl. This shattered relationship may lead her to become embittered against men in general, thus depriving herself of future relationships. Sadly some young women become convinced that sex is the only way she can garner a boy's attention. She may become promiscuous in a terrible mix of a wish for intimacy and a desire to punish herself.

Truly, the way of the world claims that sex is a tool you have to please yourself, even if that pleasure comes at the expense of others. Therefore, the following themes are considered true in the world today:

- Postponing sex until marriage is a foolish act of depriving yourself of pleasure. You should feel free to have sex when you want.

- It's cool to look as sexually adventurous as possible. (Just ask Britney Spears and Christina Aguilera, or whatever girl has most recently been persuaded to take off most of her clothes to sell more CDs.)

- It's okay for teenagers to have sex when they feel ready to do it. This means that they know better than God when it's right to engage in sex.

- Multiple sexual partners are a good idea because you deserve the experience.

- Clothing should be designed to make you look more sexually desirable.

- Adultery is justifiable if someone is not getting what he or she wants from a spouse. (Some people make the same argument for prostitution.)

- Abortion should empower young women to have sex without worrying about the burden of an unwanted child.

- Feminism teaches young women that sex is a weapon to be used by women in order to gain control over men.

The list goes on and on. The world's attitude toward sex (that it's a tool to be used for selfish pleasure) is perpetuated in magazines, beer commercials, sitcoms, fashion, popular music, and more. We live in a very sexualized world, where all—especially youth—are conditioned to believe that promiscuity is a good thing. Meanwhile, modesty, purity, and virginity are derided and scorned as prudish, weird, and unnatural to the point where it's hard to see them as treasured virtues.

It's quite the contrast when it comes to sex. God declares sex a powerful gift to be used in marriage for the purpose of servanthood. This is not to say that within marriage sex becomes a drudgery that a husband and wife have to go through—another false teaching of the world. As long as both partners approach sex as servants to one another, it remains a source of intimacy and pleasure. The world says that sex is a powerful tool for you to use in whatever way selfishly gratifies you. Any use of sex outside of God's will is selfishness. Homosexuality selfishly rejects the Lord's clear law for a perverted desire. In the end, arguments about genetics and "being born that way" don't matter—what matters is what God's Word says.

> *Therefore God gave them up in the lusts of their hearts to impurity, to the dishonoring of their bodies among themselves, because they exchanged the truth about God for a lie and worshiped and served the creature rather than the Creator, who is blessed forever! Amen. For this reason God gave them up to dishonorable passions. For their women exchanged natural relations for those that are contrary to nature; and the men likewise gave up natural relations with women and were consumed with passion for one another, men committing shameless acts with men and receiving in themselves the due penalty for their error. And since they did not see fit to acknowledge God, God gave them up to a debased mind to do what ought not to be done. They were filled with all manner of unrighteousness, evil, covetousness, malice. They are full of envy, murder, strife, deceit, maliciousness. They are gossips, slanderers, haters of God, insolent,*

haughty, boastful, inventors of evil, disobedient
to parents, foolish, faithless, heartless, ruthless.
Though they know God's decree that those who
practice such things deserve to die, they not only
do them but give approval to those who practice
them. ROMANS 1:24–32

Pornography is certainly a selfish act. The one who indulges imagines having sex with another without their consent—such mental adultery is hardly a selfless action. "But I say to you that everyone who looks at a woman with lustful intent has already committed adultery with her in his heart" (Matthew 5:28). Likewise, masturbation is clearly a matter of self-gratification, or—as the world spins it—"self-love." The lure of the world becomes unavoidable. The Old Adam in each one of us lives by selfishness with lust a nearly universal temptation. Given that, I offer the following arguments for saving sex until marriage.

1. GOD SAYS SO.

That ought to be enough right there. For starters, you have the Sixth Commandment, "Thou shall not commit adultery" (Exodus 20:14). Luther's explanation in the *Small Catechism* says it quite well, "We should fear and love God that we may lead a sexually pure and decent life in what we say and do, and husband and wife love and honor each other" (p. 10). As those set free from sin in order to live by God's Word, the Sixth Commandment should be sufficient. But if you want more, for starters check out Hebrews 13:4; Galatians 5:19; 1 Corinthians 6:16–20; Ephesians 5:1–7; Colossians 3:1–5; and 1 Thessalonians 4:2–5.

2. GOD SAYS SO FOR A REASON—consider the consequences.

The consequences of extramarital sex are astonishing. A sampling of the troubles follows:

a. First, immorality cheapens you. Remember the dialogue at the beginning of this chapter between Robert and Sally about the used engagement ring? The more times Robert gave it away, the more damaged and less meaningful it became. It might have still meant something to him, or not. In any event, it lost all of its precious uniqueness. I don't think it's any girl's dream to receive an engagement ring that a guy has already given to four other girls. As precious as a diamond ring might be, it is nothing in comparison to you—and to your body. A diamond ring is a bit of rock and metal that does nothing; your body is a gift of God with the power to create more life. A diamond ring can be replaced; in this world, your body cannot.

The world would have you believe that you should guard your possessions more and yourself less. Occasionally I work with couples living together outside of marriage. I am utterly astonished that they will keep separate bank accounts, CD and video collections, and titles to cars, yet freely connect their bodies together as if it were no big thing. Why would people entrust their bodies to someone else to whom they won't even entrust their CD collection? If sex is cheapened enough in a relationship where the two actually try to commit to each other, how much more devaluing is the "freedom" of casual sex. Such sexual activity—the world calls it "freedom"—does not increase one's worth. Just the opposite! Sarah Hinlicky writes,

> *"So-called sexual freedom is really just proclaiming oneself to be available for free, and therefore without value. To 'choose' such freedom is tantamount to saying that one is worth nothing . . . . The dark reality, of course, is that it is not free choice at all when women must convince men to love them and must convince themselves that they are more than just 'used goods.' There are so many young women I have known for whom freely chosen sexual activity means a brief moment of pleasure—if that—followed by the unchosen side effects of self-hatred that is*

impenetrable by feminist analysis. So-called sexual freedom is really just proclaiming oneself to be available for free, and therefore without value. To 'choose' such freedom is tantamount to saying that one is worth nothing." ("SUBVERSIVE VIRGINITY," *FIRST THINGS*, OCTOBER 1998, PAGES 14–16.)

On my way to church I drive past a house that often has a pile of stuff with a sign that says "Free to whoever wants it." It's free because it's worthless stuff that nobody wants. To give your body away "for free" in promiscuous sex is to declare that you have no worth. This contradicts what the Lord says of you, that you're worth the price of His Son's blood. Furthermore, in an attempt to bury guilt, you might be tempted to be more promiscuous, which in the end will only leave you feeling more worthless. Lots of people will tell you that depression may lead to promiscuity, but it's equally true that promiscuity leads to depression. Being popular by being promiscuous is like being popular by having a party where you give everyone whatever they want to eat and drink. As soon as it's no longer available, they go somewhere else and you're not popular anymore. They're friends as long as they can selfishly use you. They're not really friends at all.

While the diamond ring analogy demonstrates how the misuse of sex cheapens you, it falls far short of demonstrating other risks and consequences. We move on . . .

b. The physical risks and consequences of sexual immorality are staggering. It's only logical to assume that promiscuous people have sex with other promiscuous people. During the focus on AIDS in the late eighties, we heard over and over that "When you have sex with someone, you have sex with everyone they've ever had sex with." Not exactly a charming thought. Sexually-transmitted diseases are easily spread—even the use of condoms is no guarantee—they can prove to be an ongoing irritant for life, or worse. Gonorrhea readily passes from mother to child during birth. Chlamydia stealthily inflames a girl's fallopian tubes without her knowledge, until years later when she discovers that she cannot have children. AIDS destroys your body. A doctor once told me, "Forget all the other warnings about sexual promiscuity and focus on this one: It can kill you!"

c. Another devastating result of sexual immorality is an unplanned and unwanted pregnancy. Despite the sinful rebellion against God, He still permits life to be conceived. Yet the prospective "parents" may see the child as a punishment and curse, not a blessing.

The fact remains that a child conceived in immorality is still a miraculous gift of God, and as such, one to be served. Those who choose to keep such a child gain a keen understanding of consequences and responsibility as they sacrifice their life's dreams in order to care for the child. Those who give up the child for adoption often spend their life wondering what might have been, for they have given away one they were given to serve. Those who choose to end the child's life by abortion add *murder* to their list of sins, selfishly selecting their own convenience over the *life* of another human being. The sin of abortion often haunts young women with its enormity of guilt and horror.

d. The mental and emotional consequences are astonishing as well. God writes His Law upon the hearts of man (Romans 2:15). The misuse of a gift as powerful as sex is bound to have an effect. The *best* mental and emotional consequence that one can hope for is shame. This means that the conscience is still at work to move the sinner to repentance, confession, and absolution.

On the other hand, shame apart from repentance causes crippling despair and deep depression. This depression results in anger at oneself if not healed by absolution. Unhealed anger either gnaws deeper or blunts the conscience until it no longer seems like sin anymore. Then, out of self-hatred or a desire to justify the behavior, the person may engage in sex more frequently. Furthermore, instead of turning the anger inward upon oneself, sometimes the person grows to despise members of the opposite sex—seeing them only as tools to be manipulated and rejected. The more one indulges in promiscuous sex, the more they train themselves in selfishness and distrust of others, thus crippling themselves and making it difficult ever to have a meaningful marriage relationship.

At one of my summer jobs during college, there was a young Christian co-ed and a guy who didn't mind boasting of his sexual conquests. He began to woo the girl, flattering her with time, attention, and gifts until she consented to sex. With her body, she also offered up her heart. And the next morning, she was even more devoted to him. However, the conquest over, the guy was ready to move on and refused even to speak to her. Emotionally devastated, she left her job shortly thereafter. Through his actions the young man taught this young lady that her only worth was to loan out certain body parts, which would then be paid off with rejection. Along with the spiritual guilt that the girl had to contend with, she also dealt with the psychological trauma of such an intimate betrayal. Indeed, many young women become so conditioned by this kind of treatment they believe their purpose is only to satisfy the sexual needs of men and expect nothing in return.

Here's a question: Who's to blame? The world denounces Christianity for reducing women simply to baby-making machines. Given what we've just looked at back in Chapter 1 such an accusation is a ridiculous lie. On the other hand, the world identifies low self-esteem in girls as the real problem. Then it goes on to encourage these same girls to wear clothing with the lowest neckline and highest hemline possible. Even as they decry the treatment of women sexually by men, feminists encourage women to use sex as a tool to manipulate men. In other words, the world attempts to tell women that they are not just good for sex, then encourages them to dress up and act as if they are only good for sex. See any hypocrisy there? Do you really want to take your cues from the world?

e. Finally, in addition to the issues we've already discussed, sexual immorality inflicts immense spiritual harm as well. First off, the one who justifies sexual immorality declares God wrong when He prohibits it. Furthermore, while we spoke of the cheapening effect of immorality, it becomes more than a denial of self-worth, but a denial of God's love. St. Paul writes: "Flee from sexual immorality. Every other sin a person commits is outside the body, but the sexually immoral person sins against his own body. Or do you not know that your body is a temple of the Holy Spirit within you, whom you have from God? You are not your own, for you were bought with a price. So glorify God in your body" (1 Corinthians 6:18–20). To indulge in sexual license denies the sacrifice of Christ to free you from such sins. Few sins drive a believer away from the faith more quickly than immorality. Why? Because those who commit sexual immorality have one of two choices: Repent and be forgiven, or remain unrepentant out of guilt, lust, or devotion to a partner. If they remain impenitent, they remain unforgiven. They won't want to hear the Word about righteousness, innocence and blessedness, so they'll start skipping church. The split is inevitable without repentance. A couple who lives together without marriage may attend church for a while. Sooner or later, however, the pastor becomes aware of their situation and as a faithful servant of God speaks to them about their living arrangement. Any pastor who has done so will tell you that the response is frequently angry, as if the pastor's to blame for telling them what God says. Without repentance, the couple likely never returns to that congregation.

All of this serves to harden the heart.

Within God's plan of marriage, sex is intended as a blessed, powerful treasure. Outside of marriage, the consequences can be astounding—more than enough to cast serious doubt on the arguments of the world. But, we add one more argument for virginity until marriage:

3. THE WORLD IS LYING.

This ought to be clear from the start because the world constantly downplays the consequences of sexual immorality. Television and movie characters hop into bed on a regular basis, rarely with any sort of consequence for their sin. Mass media tends to portray promiscuous men and women as triumphant go-getters with no regrets. The campaign for AIDS funding acknowledges that AIDS is transmitted primarily through sexual contact; however, it demands that a cure be found when chastity alone would nearly halt the disease in its tracks.

The world lies, and here's why: Darkness hates light because light exposes the darkness.

> *For everyone who does wicked things hates the light and does not come to the light, lest his deeds should be exposed.* JOHN 3:20

But sexual immorality and all impurity or covetousness must not even be named among you, as is proper among saints. Let there be no filthiness nor foolish talk nor crude joking, which are out of place, but instead let there be thanksgiving. For you may be sure of this, that everyone who is sexually immoral or impure, or who is covetous (that is, an idolater), has no inheritance in the kingdom of Christ and God. Let no one deceive you with empty words, for because of these things the wrath of God comes upon the sons of disobedience. Therefore do not associate with them; for at one time you were darkness, but now you are light in the Lord. Walk as children of light (for the fruit of light is found in all that is good and right and true), and try to discern what is pleasing to the Lord. Take no part in the unfruitful works of darkness, but instead expose them. For it is shameful even to speak of the things that they do in secret. But when anything is exposed by the light, it becomes visible, for anything that becomes visible is light. Therefore it says, "Awake, O sleeper, and arise from the dead, and Christ will shine on you." Look carefully then how you walk, not as unwise but as wise, making the best use of the time, because the days are evil. Therefore do not be foolish, but understand what the will of the Lord is. EPHESIANS 5:3–17

Guilt hates innocence because innocence shows what guilt is, or better yet, what guilt is not. Impurity hates purity. Sin hates righteousness. The world hates the things of God. Thus St. Paul writes in Colossians:

> *Set your minds on things that are above, not on things that are on earth. For you have died, and your life is hidden with Christ in God. When Christ who is your life appears, then you also will appear with Him in glory. Put to death therefore what is earthly in you: sexual immorality, impurity, passion, evil desire, and covetousness, which is idolatry.* COLOSSIANS 3:2–5

This may sound strange, but I believe it to be true. The number one reason that the world wants you to engage in sexual immorality is so that it can feel better about itself. It wants you to lose your virginity because it can't regain its virginity. Remember, at the heart of immorality lies selfishness, and the selfish world doesn't like being accused by examples of purity. The world will coax you to become "one of them," saying that you should enjoy sexual freedom. This is simply a lie. Sexual immorality entraps you within the bondage of sin, not freedom. The world desires you to become "one of them" so that your innocence no longer accuses them of their guilt.

All of this should come as no surprise. When Jesus was crucified, His enemies mocked Him for exactly who He was—the pure, sinless Son of God. Christians are the Bride of Christ, the Church. Through the sacrifice of Jesus, the Church is described as "sanctified," "cleansed," and "without spot or wrinkle or any such thing, that she might be holy and without blemish" (Ephesians 5:27b). The world mocks the Church even as it scorns the Lord; therefore, the world will mock anyone who seeks to follow God's Word and remain sexually pure until marriage. Sexual purity accuses them of all their sin—spiritual immorality—against God. Sexual immorality, on the other hand, involves the horrible abuse of a powerful gift of God in order to turn people away from the God who gave it.

Note also that many of the false gods (Baal, Asherah, Ishtar, etc.) which troubled Israel in the Bible were fertility cults, in which sexual immorality and temple prostitution were part of worship. In college and elsewhere, you'll run into theologians and anthropologists who will tell you that such fertility cults resulted from man's fascination with the "mysterious" origin of life. But this misses the mark. Since God revealed Himself as the origin of life in His Word, the origin of life is no mystery for the

Christian, for life is found only in Christ. No, such practices were sinful man's selfish perversion of God's gift of sex into rebellion against Him.

The world lies about sex yet again when it declares that the Church opposes *all* sexual behavior as somehow "dirty." This is simply not true. In accordance with God's Word, Christians believe that sex is a gift from God, given for a specific time and place—marriage. God gives certain gifts for specific situations. Electricity provides wondrous blessings, but I'd caution you against taking a radio into the bathtub with you. Gasoline performs wonders as it powers our cars, but don't mix it into tonight's casserole. Sex has a place, and it's called marriage. "Therefore a man shall leave his father and his mother and hold fast to his wife, and they shall become one flesh" (Genesis 2:24). For it is within marriage that sex becomes a blessing from God. Given the consequences of immorality and the blessings God promises for those who follow His Word, sex is definitely worth the wait.

While this book is intended to talk about dating, we might as well throw in a quick note about premarital cohabitation—a.k.a. living together without the benefit of marriage—a rampant behavior among couples in the world today. No matter the excuse used to justify cohabitation, it comes back to selfishness over servanthood. For instance:

"We thought it would be better for our marriage if we saw how things worked before we went ahead and got married." This sounds good, except that studies consistently show that those who live together first suffer higher divorce rates later on. Individuals make this excuse while trying to justify a selfish act against sound empirical data.

"We want to get married, but we can't afford to do it financially right now." Translated, this means, "Money is more important to us than God's command."

"Everybody's doing it" gets low marks for lack of creativity, although it's often expressed as "Times have changed and it's socially acceptable now." Translated, this means, "Society agrees with our selfish desires that are condemned by God's Word, and that's good enough for us." It's selfish and immature again, and deserves an immature response like, "If society jumped off a cliff, would you?"

"We love each other." Since love is based upon servanthood and self-sacrifice, the couple that makes this claim isn't computing very well as living together is based on selfishness. If their love is truly based upon the Lord's love for them, then their actions will be in accordance with His will.

"We live together, but we're not having sex." Even *if* this were true, Christians are commanded to avoid the appearance of evil. "Do all things without grumbling or questioning, that you may be blameless and innocent, children of God without blemish in the midst of a crooked and twisted generation, among whom you shine as lights in the world, holding fast to the word of life, so that in the day of Christ I may be proud that I did not run in vain or labor in vain" (Philippians 2:14–16).

"We're putting others first, and waiting to set a wedding date when everybody can come." Translated, this means, "We selfishly refused to wait to start living together; everybody else will just have to catch up."

The list goes on, and would almost be amusing |if so much weren't at stake. The couple that chooses to live together places their relationship and salvation in grave danger.

virginity restored:
hope for those
who have sinned

chapter

eight

chapter eight

It would be naïve to write about sex and think that all who read or hear this are still virgins.

For those who have indulged in sexual immorality, the previous chapter concerning the consequences cannot be pleasant to sit through. If that includes you, I do not intend offense. I also assume that this book will be read by those who still preserve their virginity. I wish to warn them of the realistic consequences of promiscuity and extol the benefits of purity. Frankly, the talk of consequences may bother you because you found them painfully accurate. The reality exists that even if you *haven't* lost your virginity, you *have* sinned against the Sixth Commandment. The Law of God always accuses.

I encourage you to rejoice in the Good News of Jesus Christ, whose blood cleanses you of all of your sins. In terms of the physical body, once lost virginity cannot be restored. However, the forgiveness Christ won, through His death and resurrection, has removed your sin from you. In Him, you stand before God, holy and without blemish—a virgin once more. When Ephesians 5 speaks of the Church as Christ's bride, the bride does not start out holy, but rather, blemished and impure, until Christ cleanses her. On different occasions Jesus speaks with women caught in immorality (John 4:7–42; Luke 7:37–50) and forgives them. While others still question their character, Jesus sends them in peace because their sin is gone.

I remember a pastor who performed a marriage for a couple where the bride was obviously pregnant. Members of the congregation criticized him because they thought that his participation in the wedding made the couple's immorality seem excusable. Instead—with the couple's permission—the pastor announced the couple confessed their sin and were forgiven. Their guilt was gone; it was the duty of the pastor and congregation to defend their right to marry in the church.

That's the power of forgiveness, won by Christ at the cross. Though sexual sins have a particular way of goading with guilt, the Lord removes them with His grace. It is why we rejoice to sing the offertory, "Create in me a clean heart, O God, and renew a right spirit within me" (Psalm 51:10). Through His means of grace, the Lord creates clean hearts and renews right spirits. Does your conscience still accuse you of a sin that you have confessed? God's Word is more sure than your conscience, and the Lord declares, "Come now, let us reason together, says the LORD: though your sins are like scarlet, they shall be as white as snow; though they are red like crimson, they shall become like wool" (Isaiah 1:18). For the sake of Jesus, you *are* forgiven and of great worth. In the sight of God, you are pure. Go in peace.

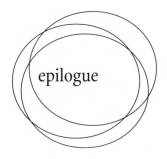

epilogue

One Final Thought

One time when I took a girl out on a first date, we went to a movie that wasn't showing. I'd used the Wednesday paper and the times had changed by Friday. The movie had moved on—about 30 miles down the road. We drove the extra half-hour and bought tickets for the next show, which started in about an hour and a half. Left with scattered showers and very few options, we spent the time at one of those well-known dating hot spots—a tropical fish store. We struggled trying to keep the conversation going, getting to know each other instead of silently staring at a screen. We finally saw the movie and I drove her home before driving back to my place. Two hundred sixty miles, one movie, and a bunch of neon tetras later, the date was over. Not a whole lot had gone according to plan.

The next day, I wrote her a letter and billed her at 28 cents per mile.

Nah, just kidding. Sinful and cheap though I may be, I'm not quite that stupid. Actually, I asked her out again. The next time we went on a day hike at a state park. At least we tried, but after a half mile or so our shoes and socks were covered with burrs and thorns that were slowly working their way into our feet. We decided that the first date had actually gone better.

But we went out again because I'd discovered something significant about her. She was the kind of girl who would go the extra mile in order to make things work out as well as they could. Rather than toss blame or call it quits, she avoided the selfish route and went for servanthood instead. As time went on, if we had an argument, she'd stick around to make sure that it got resolved. She was willing to work at making things work, so eventually I bought an engagement ring. Like so many of our dates, the proposal went exactly *not* according to plan, but she said yes anyway. We've been married for thirteen years now, and I think she still likes me, which is pretty cool.

Thirteen years later, we're still forgiven saints and selfish sinners. Each day, we still see that selfishness wants to give servanthood the boot so we try to keep serving, confessing, and forgiving as top priorities. All of this is by the grace of God, found in the Son of Man who "came not to be served but to serve, and to give His life as a ransom for many" (Matthew 20:28).

As a young adult, I don't expect you to take this book with you when you go out on a date. Though if you do, at least you'll have something to read if you go to a movie that isn't showing and the tropical fish store is closed. But I do hope you'll keep this in mind. In any relationship, it will always be the battle of selfishness versus servanthood. However, the stakes are never higher than when you start to date someone seriously. You may well commit yourself to serving them for a lifetime.

You don't know—can't know—when dating will turn into serious dating with a future mate. So remember who you are, and *whose* you are. You're a forgiven child of God because the Son of God served you through His death and resurrection. He continues to serve you by daily forgiving your sins. Delivered from sin, you're set free to be a servant to others, and that servanthood will never be more important than with the mate you have for life. So date wisely, and find someone who wants to be a servant, too.

Even though servanthood goes a long way, you don't know what lies ahead, and there are no guarantees of lifelong happiness. So rejoice in Christ, your Bridegroom, who ransomed you by His cross and remains faithful. Always! No matter what happens, you can be certain of His love and faithfulness.